No Permits Issued Today

BISHOP ROSETTE CONEY

No Permits issued Today Copyright © 2017 by Bishop Rosette Coney Published in the United States of America by Gospel 4 U Network

All Rights Reserved. No part of this book may be reproduced or transmitted in anyway by means, electronic, mechanical, Photocopy, recording or otherwise, without prior permission of the author except as provided by USA copyright law.

Scriptures are taken from the King James Version of the **Holy Bible** unless otherwise marked.
ISBN – 978-0-9984665-4-5
Library of Congress Number – 2017946760
Printed in United States of America
June 2017

Content

Dedication

Foreword

Acknowledgement

Introduction

DON'T GIVE PERMISSION FOR...

Chapter 1 - Your Determination to be Broken ------17

Chapter 2 - Your Spirit to be Crushed......................23

Chapter 3 - Your Self Esteem to be Smashed--------29

Chapter 4 - Your Enthusiasm to be Silenced---------35

Chapter 5 - Your Identity to be Stolen----------------41

Chapter 6 - Your Health to Fail-----------------------45

Chapter 7 - Your Joy to be Removed-----------------53

Chapter 8 - Your Feelings to be Hurt-----------------59

Chapter 9 - Your Smile to be Reversed---------------65

Chapter 10 - Your Blessings to be Blocked----------75

Chapter 11 - Your Mind to Become Polluted--------81

Chapter 12 - Your Vision to be Aborted--------------89

Chapter 13 - Your Heart to be Discouraged----------95

Chapter 14 - Your Past to Infect Your Future--------101

Scriptural Encouragement for Strength---------------109

About the Author

Dedication

I dedicate this book to those who haven't been able to get a handle on their actions or reactions to negative attacks by Satan through circumstances or other people; those who's spirits have been crushed by the spirit of Satan, operating through people who despise them without a cause, who are jealous of them because of their success or envy them because of their positive influence on others. It is my desire to turn their focus in a direction that will bring out a positive - not negative response to challenging situations. This will protect their Godly character, empower them and point them in a non-interrupted direction towards their destiny and will ultimately bring glory to God.

I dedicate this book to the Almighty God, who has empowered me to cancel the issuance of all permits - TODAY!

Acknowledgement

First and foremost, I acknowledge the Almighty God, who is most certainly my everything. He has empowered me to realize who I am and Whose I am in every aspect of my life, while keeping me humbled enough to recognize and realize that I am absolutely nothing without Him.

I acknowledge the giants in my life; the spiritual leaders whom He allowed me to sit under long enough in order to catch a glimpse of their anointing. Just one drop of the oil of their wisdom, knowledge, charm, experience and tenacity has pushed me forward into the destiny carved out for me. I thank you all for that...*and you know who you are!*

I have been placed in a position - through my own personal experiences, where I can boldly take charge of my feelings and not issue any permits for people or circumstances to hurt me, walk all over me, cancel my dreams or kill my visions. If I issue permits to people or situations, soon they will want a license to drive me plum crazy. I resolve that no permits will be issued today! No, not today!

I acknowledge my wonderful family; my dedicated husband, Gene, my wonderful children Tamika (Norman), Anitra (Menan) and my precious grandchildren Makayla, Tamia and Aaron. I sure do love you guys and pray that you will never issue permits to people, places or things for them to hurt you in any way.

I acknowledge my aunt, Mother Anna Lee Green; who even at the age of 103, continues to be the inspiring queen of the family - exemplifying wisdom, beauty and charm. You have demonstrated so much strength and stamina that we can't help but be strong. I praise my God for you Aunt Lee!

To my sisters, Faye (John) and Sharon (Horace); thank you for being my guideposts, propping me up on both sides as we continue to sing God's praises together.

I acknowledge the endearing flock that I pastor for their love and dedication in all things. You hold a special place in my heart and I encourage you to continue growing strong, in spite of your challenges. I truly love you!

I thank all of you who are connected to me in any area of my life. I love you.

BISHOP ROSETTE CONEY

Foreword

Praise the name of our Lord Jesus;

Bishop Coney has indeed written a book that encourages the reader to grow in the Lord. In our churches, there are many who find themselves controlled by others and that action of control can make the Christian life frustrating at times. "No More Permits" will cause the reader to take control of their lives and refuse to allow others to influence the course of their lives.

I enjoyed reading this book as it focuses on the removal of the blame-shifting that is so prevalent in our culture. We often blame others for our shortcomings and our failures. After reading, "No More Permits" you will develop a winning attitude that will resonate deep within your spirit. I believe that our God wants us to prosper and be in health as our soul prospers (*III John*). This book will start you on the road to spiritual maturity and the joy of setting boundaries for your life.

In the Holy Scriptures, we read of those who attempt to defeat the people of God, and they were turned away by the power of the Holy Spirit. We find ourselves in that position today. Many believers are defeated by the words and attitudes of others long before they even enter the battle. Just as the children of Israel assumed that they could not defeat the "ites" that were in the land of promise, we often find ourselves defeated before we even try to win. We give others permission to set the boundaries for our lives and thereby bring us to defeat.

Bishop Rosette Coney brings a new level of renewed purpose and excitement as she walks you through the steps of successful living. I have found that Bishop Coney truly lives what she preaches, sings and writes. I wholeheartedly endorse the message of this book, and I trust that you will be blessed reading "No More Permits." When you complete this book, you will discover that people can only exercise control over you if you give them permission to do so. When you realize your place in God, you will then seek to eliminate the level of control others have over you.

Throughout this book these facts emerge:

- Trust the Lord to control your life.
- Study the Word of God regularly to know what the Lord promises you.
- Rejoice in the relationship that you have with the Lord Jesus.
- Forgive others and walk in victory.

Bishop Rosette Coney has hit a home run with the thought, "No More Permits." I am convinced that each of us will walk in the freedom and joy of the Lord Jesus when we stop giving others permission to control our lives and our responses.

Blessings to all who read.

Eric A. Lambert, Jr.

Bishop Eric A. Lambert, Jr.

Presiding Bishop

Bethel Deliverance International Fellowship of Churches

BISHOP ROSETTE CONEY

Introduction

"No Permits Issued Today"
An Empowering Tool

This book is written to encourage anyone experiencing challenges in various areas of life when encountering others who are influenced by negative sources and attack them socially, emotionally, psychologically, spiritually, mentally and in some cases – physically. This book is also for those faced with situations which keep them from moving forward in their lives.

I have a burden for people who are intentionally hurt by others who don't take the time to get to know them or understand them. There is a great need to empower people (who are bullied in some way) to know how to connect with the God-given strength they have inside of them and tap into that internal peace provided by the great promise of Jesus; *"These things I have spoken unto you, that in me ye might have peace. In the world ye shall have tribulation:*

but be of good cheer; I have overcome the world." (John 16:33 KJV)

There are also situations and circumstances which arise in people's lives that can almost paralyze them - such as the death of a loved one, being terminated from employment, the breakup of marriages or relationships or even those who experience sicknesses or a change in their physical condition. Apostle Paul offers instructions to strengthen our minds; *"Let this mind be in you, which was also in Christ Jesus:"*(Philippians 2:5 KJV). Paul entertained thoughts of good will, thoughts of healing, thoughts of deliverance, thoughts of prayers to His Heavenly Father, thoughts of increase, thoughts of wisdom, thoughts of humility, thoughts of resurrection, thoughts of the glorious new and not the dreadful old.

I introduce this book to assist readers with feeling good about themselves in spite of what others say or think, or in spite of situations that shatter their hopes for a bright future. Get ready to explore other techniques and avenues of how to silently reject traps set by Satan with the ability to boldly recognize the attacks and avoid reaction.

Enjoy the opportunity to change for the better and say out loud with me, *"**No permits issued today!**"*

Chapter 1

Don't Give Permission For...

... *Your Determination to be Broken*

First of all, let me define the word determination; Determination is firmness of purpose; resoluteness. I believe that each of us were born with a seed of determination. That determination caused us to position ourselves to push from our mother's womb - the small area of space which housed us for nine months and entrapped us like a worm, waiting to become a butterfly.

Once we were born, that seed of determination was watered with desires and life experiences. As we grew, the seed of determination began to grow within us - pushing us forward with determination to reach towards our destiny. We left the cushiony comfort of our mother's womb behind us - we left the cocoon and pressed forward into the form of a beautiful butterfly. Apostle Paul said it this way; *"Brethren, I count not myself to have apprehended: but this one thing I do , forgetting those things which are behind, and reaching forth unto those things which are before, I press toward the mark for the prize of the high calling of God in Christ Jesus."* (Philippians 3:13-14 KJV)

Determination is pressing. Determination is pushing through curtains of tears. Determination is enduring hardness as a good soldier of Jesus Christ. Yes, determination is continuing when you really want to stop. I remember times when I became tired of the lies, tired of the misunderstandings, being misjudged, criticized and scrutinized. I had many days when I wanted to throw in the towel, but my determination made my pain seem minimal in size.

I recall when my husband and oldest daughter were injured in a horrible life- threatening accident and how there was great possibility they could have lost their lives. With a determined mind, I told the devil, "No Permits Issued

Today". I told him I would not permit him to kill my family, my faith in the healing power of the Almighty God, my dedication and commitment to the service of God's kingdom, nor my spirit. With a determined mind, I never missed my church services while they were hospitalized; I went to work praying they would be guarded by the Angels of God when I could not be there to hold their hands - and they were. Those angels were on duty every moment and every second of every day!

Listen, you have the steering wheel in your hands to direct your determination. Steer yourself into your destiny - avoiding any distractions that may hinder your determination. No one or any situation should be permitted to break your determination.

There is a hitman out there (Satan) waiting to break your determination, but you really have to work hard to keep him at bay. Follow these practices to keep your determination from being broken:

1. Develop realistic and attainable goals - goals that are within your reach. This will keep you from becoming discouraged along the way.

2. Develop a 'to-do' list and write down tasks and goals for each day. It feels good when you can cross off completed projects. Become determined to complete the items on your list by the end of a designated timeframe.

3. Celebrate yourself when you reach the desired goal. Go shopping within reason.

4. Give yourself space and time between projects.

5. Never beat yourself up when you feel you haven't met your mark. Just keep on trying until you've reached the desired goal(s).

6. Be determined to read and study about those who have gone before you, leaving a path of accomplishments for you to strive for.

7. Don't allow any distraction to come between you and your determination. Make yourself a guaranteed winner!

8. Keep reaching for higher marks each time you accomplish your goal.

9. Be determined to keep your body in shape so that you will be fit and ready to complete your life-long goals.

10. Motivate yourself by music playing while you are working.

11. Pump yourself up and become your best cheerleader. Others will see your enthusiasm and determination and will become motivated to do better themselves.

12. Develop good living habits like going to bed early, drinking plenty of water and visiting your doctors regularly.

I share with you a quote from Tony Evans' book, *Destiny*; *"God has designed you to have all that you need to productively rule your world."* Now, just rule that world God generously gave you with a strong determination to accomplish and meet all of your personal goals without any more excuses.

Go on out there! Write that book. Sing that song. Build that house. Buy that car. Have that baby. Land that job. Grab your life and run the path already cut out for you. There's nothing in your way. Be determined and confident that you can and will do all things through Christ, who continues to give you daily strength for every mountain you have to climb. His presence will be felt and you will have confidence that the Lord is with you.

"*...and, lo, I am with you always, even unto the end of the world. Amen.*" Matthew 28:20 (KJV)

Now, say out loud with me, "***No permits issued today to break my determination!***"

Chapter 2

Don't Give Permission For...

... *Your Spirit to be Crushed*

Your spirit is your inner self. Your spirit is the nonphysical part of you - it is the seat of your emotions and character; it is the soul of you. Your spirit is where those qualities regarded as forming the definitive or typical elements in your character are housed.

When your spirits are high, your production is high. When your production is high, what you receive from your production is high. When what you receive is high, your visibility is high. When your visibility is high, the attacks lunged against you are high. You become a very good target for haters to aim their weapons of destruction.

People who are intimidated by you will rise up from their dormancy and do all they can to crush your spirits. They will try to kill out that drive in you; that magnificent motivation; that electrifying charisma; that joyful and positive attitude you have. They will make every attempt to form in you a type of failure component that will crush your motivational spirit, thus rendering you helpless and without enough spirit to bounce back from the multiple attacks. They come to kick you out of the boxing ring of success. They want to sit on you, pounce on you and stomp out your spirit.

"The thief cometh not, but for to steal, and to kill, and to destroy:" John 10:10 (KJV)

I advise you not to give anyone permission to crush your spirit. Your spirit was made to soar, not to be caged in fear. No one except the Almighty God has power over you, and this knowledge is only reserved for those of you who know who they are and who's they are. No one can crush your spirit unless you give them permission to do so. I think of a wonderful man I met on my Hawaii cruise. His name was Ulysses, and he was an interesting character. He was a veteran Army Official, a retired school teacher, a fabulous father, and so much more. I was astounded by the wisdom, knowledge and strength this man had, with such a strong zeal for life, even at the age of 88 plus years old. Only a few years ago, he lost his wife of over sixty plus years, Dorothy, and he spoke of her as though she was still living inside of him. He joyfully shared with my husband and I of the good times he and his wife had traveling all over the world while she lived. His face would light up when he spoke of her - such love between a man and woman is rarely found. As much as he loved his wife, he did not let her passing crush his spirit. He continued to enjoy life to the fullest and continued traveling all over the world, now with his devoted daughter, Karen. They were the best of friends who always had each other's backs. Ulysses encouraged Gene and I to always love and appreciate each other, because you never know when you will be separated by death. Although this retiree lives alone in Orlando, FL, he never has a dull moment because he stays busy donating his time for the cause in the field of education. He sits on boards where his wisdom and knowledge can be appreciated and impacting, and he travels to various conventions every year. Yes, the core of his spirit, his lovely wife, Dorothy, passed away years ago, but Ulysses has a determination not to let his spirit die with her. He survived three aneurysms, and he lives on; still laughing, still traveling, still impacting, still inspiring, high-spirited, with a healthy appetite to eat whatever is placed in front of him. Like Ulysses, you have to determine within yourself that a crushed spirit, a heavy heart, gloom and doom is just not going to happen today. There will be no permits issued for spirit crushing today.

When your spirit is crushed, you become paralyzed. You can't move forward - you are in the "stand still" mode. When your spirit is crushed you constantly tell yourself, "I can't do it! I just can't go on!" I dare to contradict that declaration, and I dare you to thrust forward with the powerful statement of Apostle Paul as recorded in Philippians 4:13 - *"I can do all things through Christ which strengtheneth me."* Barak Obama planted a seed in all of us when, as a black man, he became President of the United States of America for two terms. They said it couldn't be done, but our former President said, Yes we can!"

When your spirit is non-functional, you're simply dead. You are of no use. You need to wake yourself up, stand up, move up, pray up, and open up your mouth and let your spirit breathe out positive statements and actions. Do not let anyone or any situation crush your spirit. Be all you can be, and be the best at being your best! Take the chains off of your spirit and get moving into the destiny already set in motion for you. Now, say out loud with me, *"**No permits issued today to crush my spirit.**"*

BISHOP ROSETTE CONEY

Chapter 3

Don't Give Permission For...

... *Your Self-Esteem to Be Smashed*

Your self-esteem is confidence in your worth or abilities – it's how well you respect yourself.

Be reminded of the fact that you are one of God's rarest and greatest creations. There is no one else like you. When God made you, He destroyed the mold. You were wonderfully and beautifully made by God, Himself. You are drop-dead, turning-head, gorgeous in His eyes! David's writings, as recorded in Psalm 139, verse 14 supports that fact, *"I will praise thee; for I am fearfully and wonderfully made: marvellous are thy works; and that my soul knoweth right well."*

Once you arrive at the level of knowing who you are, cherishing your beauty, basking in the great work you are by the hands of your Creator - the Great God, celebrating your existence; up pops the devil and his little imps, packing sledge hammers. They come to take those sledge hammers and smash your high self-esteem. They want to wipe you out with rumors, lies, insults, offenses, incidents and accidents. They want to hit you so hard until you lose your godly identity and conscientiousness - they want to knock you all the way down the steps into the basement of low self-esteem. For Satan, this is a slow, but very effective and destructive process. He wants to make you feel ugly, worthless, meaningless, and hopeless. He wants you to affirm declarations over your life out of your own mouth, with words that lower your self-esteem to the point of no return. Your tongue is so powerful that it makes you or breaks you. You become what you say.

"Death and life are in the power of the tongue: and they that love it shall eat the fruit thereof.:" Proverbs 18:21 (KJV)

Don't let anything or anyone crush your self-esteem. Take your power back by speaking positive affirmations and declarations over your life. Next to Jesus, you are the best friend you could ever have. Start telling yourself how valuable you are. Say it loud and out of your own mouth. Remind yourself of the fact that you are made from good quality dirt - a rich soil that only God could produce. Remind yourself that you are the apple of God's eye. Psalm 17:8 is where David asked God to keep him in that status. "Keep me as the apple of the eye, hide me under the shadow of thy wings,"

Don't let rejections or denials lower your self-esteem. Maybe that job just wasn't the one God had planned for you. Maybe that man or woman who walked off from you, leaving you in a curled up fetus position with a heart broken into thousands of pieces just wasn't the mate God paired you up with. Maybe that child you lost before you could deliver it would have costed you more than your emotions could afford. Maybe that car you had dreams of purchasing could have ended your life down the road in a terrible accident. Who knows? God's plan for you was developed long before you were even conceived in your mother's womb. Whatever plate life serves you on, don't let that plate turn into an iron cast skillet that becomes the item that crushes your self-esteem. Hang around positive people - people who contribute to raising your self-esteem - not self-esteem crushers.

I'm reminded of a story of an ugly little duckling that became displaced from its parents by wandering off too far from the nest. He was so ugly, they didn't bother looking for him. He wandered past a flock of pigeons on the ground that laughed at him, taunted and teased him about being so ugly. Because the ugly duckling was so lonely he continued waddling around with the pigeons and always had a low opinion of himself. He feasted off of food wasted by the pigeons, which caused them to tease him even the more. He finally had enough of that and moved on until he spotted a pack of sparrows. They thought he was the most hideous thing they had ever seen. They ran from him, laughing and ridiculing him along the way. He tried his best to keep up with them, so desperate for company, but they always kept their distance. Finally, he stumbled across some eagles who landed to get a bite to eat. They were so much larger than he was, so he hid behind some bushes and watched their every move. He did this for a couple of day, just lurking in the background. Then one day when the rain was pouring down hard upon the land, one of the eagles spotted him and hid him under their wings for protection. From that spot, he continued to observe the actions of the eagles and emulated them. He ate what they ate, he walked the way they walked with his head held high, and he even tried his wings at flying like them. He began to feel pretty good about himself. One day the eagles took flight and flew so high above the sky, the ugly duckling couldn't keep up. He felt himself getting closer and closer to the ground as the eagles soared far out of sight. The poor ugly duckling found himself on the ground again, this time among a pack of proud ducks prancing back and forth along the beach. When they saw him, he looked like a polished, properly groomed, intelligent duckling with a strong set of wings. He was able to recognize his parents and joyfully quacked his way into their presence. They were so shocked and proud of their son, who was once classified as an ugly duckling; but because he had been in good company, they hardly recognized him. He was no longer referred to as the "ugly duckling". He became powerful, popular and the leader of the pack - all because he removed himself from self-esteem crushers and transformed himself under the wings of strong self-esteem raisers. On purpose, position yourself around people with high self-esteem and those who are living out their purpose. Do not issue permits to esteem crushers -

stay clear of those kind of people, and enjoy being that wonderful person God created you to be!

I have resolved within myself not to allow anyone to smash my image of me with their name calling or evil speaking about me. When they try to make me feel like am being mistreated, I say to myself, "I am not mistreated – I am Mrs. Treated!" When they try to label me as misunderstood, I say, "I am not misunderstood – I am Mrs. Understood!" When they try to make me feel like I am misjudged, I say, "I am not misjudged – I am Mrs. Judge!" When they try to make me feel like I am misfortunate, I say, "I am not misfortunate – I am Mrs. Fortunate!" When they try to label me as misclassified, I say, "I am not misclassified – I am Mrs. Classified! I am the classiest thing out there!" You become what you say!

Now, open your mouth and say out loud with me, *"No permits issued today to smash my self-esteem!"*

Chapter 4

Don't Give Permission For...

... Your Enthusiasm to be Silenced

Your enthusiasm is your intense and eager enjoyment of something associated with your life - often displayed outwardly. Being enthusiastic is being excited! I am excited each time I come into the presence of God in the sanctuary of a church with fellow worshippers, so I give Him high praises! I jump! I shout! I sing aloud to demonstrate outwardly my enthusiasm. But I am also excited when I hear my husband's voice or his key turn in the door. Just knowing that he made it home safely gets me excited. There are so many things that can happen on his way home. Some may think this is nothing to get excited about and maybe even throw out a slight negative comment about it, with the intent of silencing my enthusiasm, but I refuse, I mean absolutely refuse to give any free permits today to silence the enthusiasm attached to the great love I have for my wonderful hubby. My excitement comes without regrets or reservations.

Now, you may have a situation, circumstance or state of affairs that threaten your enthusiasm or knock the eagerness out of you; I urge you to vehemently protect your enthusiasm, at all costs! Be excited about your life and what you're into. Proclaim it on the mountain top! Scream it in the valley. If you're in love, shout it out - scream it out - proclaim it before the whole world! Your enthusiasm is your passion - be passionate about the things that are important to you.

I know a young lady named Janeen, who is passionate about her relationship with God; and in church services, she tends to be a little loud with her hallelujahs. It doesn't matter who looks at her, who holds their ears, who laughs at her - she belts out her high-pitched voice, throws her head back and bellows her biggest "Hallelujah" in praise to her One and Only God. Janeen refuses to give any free permits out to silence her enthusiasm, because every time she thinks of the goodness of Jesus and what He has done for her, her soul cries out, Hallelujah, and she thanks God for saving her.

"And a voice came forth from the throne, saying, Give praise to our God, all ye his servants, ye that fear him, the small and the great. And I heard as it were the voice of a great multitude, and as the voice of many waters, and as the voice of mighty thunders, saying, Hallelujah: for the Lord our God, the Almighty, reigneth. Let us rejoice and be exceeding glad..." Revelation 19:5-7a (ASV)

Your enthusiasm is what keeps you passionate about everything you do. When that passion is prevalent your presentation in all that you do will be in the spirit of excellence. When you are enthusiastic, your enthusiasm should and will wear off on anyone who loves you or cares for you. But you must keep in mind that there are those who will despise your excitement and do all they can to silence you. Don't give them permission to silence you - you can do this without speaking a word. Just keep on celebrating life; just keep on praising your God; just keep on doing your best to stay on your high about everything you do, Do not allow anyone or anything to throw you in the basement regarding your emotions. Stay on the top floor with your enthusiasm. Your love for God motivates you to be enthusiastic about everything. And even when there are many attempts made against you with the intent to silence your passion, keep your mind on Jesus and ignore the attempts. The attempts are sent your way to notify you, but they will actually glorify you and the God you represent. Remain cognizant of the fact that He brings out the best in you. Now, say out loud with me, "***No permits issued today to silence my enthusiasm!***"

"If ye be reproached for the name of Christ, happy are ye; for the spirit of glory and of God resteth upon you: on their part he is evil spoken of, but on your part he is glorified." ~ 1st Peter 4:14 (KJV)

If your enthusiasm is silenced, the world cannot know how great and extremely awesome our God is - they will know His unique ability to be present in every area of their lives - they will be robbed of knowing the advantage they have in making a joyful noise unto the Lord. They will never know the fantastic blessings they can receive when they are excited about Jesus. Just the mention of His name brings life to dead situations, forces individuals to raise the hands

NO PERMITS ISSUED TODAY

in triumph and their heads to pronounce with their mouths victory and not defeat. People who are generally enthusiastic live a life of celebration. They celebrate because they were able to wake up in the morning clothed in their right minds with the use and activities of their limbs; they celebrate their going out and coming in, and they really celebrate when they are in the presence of God with the saints at church. Yes, no permits issuing people celebrate like this

C	Clap - they clap their hands to the glory of God
E	Exalt - they exalt His name forever
L	Lift - they lift their voices in laughter out loud
E	Elevate - they elevate their arms in praise
B	Beat - they beat the drums to make a loud noise
R	Rejoice - they rejoice in the sanctuary for His goodness
A	Arise - they arise from their seats to acknowledge His presence
T	Testify - they testify to others of His goodness
E	Exercise - they exercise their liberty to celebrate and they embrace others

Knowing what kind of God we serve, how on earth can you give anyone permission to silence your enthusiasm? Jump to your feet right now and declare with me, *"There will be not permits issued today to silence my transmittable enthusiasm!!"*

Chapter 5

Don't Give Permission For...

... Your Identity to Be Stolen

Your identity is your identification. It is the fact of being whom or what you are. Your identity tells people your story. It's your responsibility to protect your identity at all times. You cannot afford to have someone steal who you are from you. If it were stolen, someone else could try to become you and live out a destiny that was created custom-made only for you. Your identity was given way before you were conceived, and it was given to you by your Creator. As Tony Evans puts it, you are God's masterpiece, and He knows every fiber of your being. God created, designed and named that masterpiece.

"But now thus saith the Lord that created thee, O Jacob, and he that formed thee, O Israel, Fear not: for I have redeemed thee, I have called thee by thy name; thou art mine."Isaiah 43:1 (KJV)

Your social security number, in this earthly realm, connects you to multiple factors in your life that can either make you or break you. Your financial status could be greatly crippled, your peace of mind could be shattered, you could become a victim and prisoner of someone controlling your identification numbers in this system and your very being could be compromised. Your SSN, in a sense, is the issue of life for you here on earth. In the same manner, your heart is your spiritual Social Security Number, and you are instructed to guard it carefully. King Solomon recorded those directions in his book of Proverbs.

"Keep thy heart with all diligence; for out of it are the issues of life."Proverbs 4:23 (KJV)

Your heart stands in jeopardy of being stolen at any given point. Don't let the enemy get you to reveal the contents of your heart. Those numbers are personal and private. Don't be a fool and play into his games of trying to reveal your identity code. Once he has your identity he has you. The truth of the matter is, he can't get to your heart unless you give him permission. He's always at the front of the line, jumping ahead of God to get a permit issued to get at your pure heart. Do all you can to keep your heart locked away and out of harm's way. Jesus said, *"Blessed are the pure in heart: for they shall see God."* (Matthew 5:8)

The heart of the matter is, being who you are is the best thing you could ever be. You are not counterfeit, you are the real thing. Your heart is tucked away, deeply inside of your body. It ticks at the rhythm God made it to beat on, and it was created to last as long as you last. If it is broken or damaged your existence could be compromised.

Protect your heart and keep it pure by hiding God's word deep down in there. David said, *"Thy word have I hid in mine heart: that I might not sin against thee." (Psalm 119:11)* When the enemy or life's situations knock on the door of your heart to steal your identity, open up your mouth and loudly proclaim, "There will be no permits issued today to steal my identity"!!! Now, take time to say it again out loud with me, ***"No permits issued today to steal my identity!"***

BISHOP ROSETTE CONEY

Chapter 6
Don't Give Permission For...

... *Your Health to Fail*

Your health is your state of being free from illnesses or injuries - physically or mentally. Your health can fail due to outside afflictions placed on you or in most cases by self-infliction. You can be your own enemy. You can be the prime source of your own attacks.

Let's examine mental failure in health. Your mind is your activation mechanism. It can remain in perfect peace if you keep it turned to the right channel. Worry can shut down your mind, crippling it to the point of no return. You can wipe your mind totally out when you keep it tuned into trouble. When you switch the channel from positive to negative, your mind can go in all sorts of directions guided by the seed of worry...

- You worry about your finances

- You worry about your family

- You worry about your marriage

- You worry about your love life or the lack thereof

- You worry about being lonely

- You worry about not having enough to eat

- You worry about the clothes you wear

- You worry about your appearance (too fat/too skinny)

- You worry about worrying

NO PERMITS ISSUED TODAY

Apostle Paul gives us instructions in Philippians 4:6, *"Be careful for nothing; but in everything by prayer and supplication with thanksgiving let your requests be made known unto God. And the peace of God, which passeth all understanding, shall keep your hearts and minds through Christ Jesus."*

> Worrying is like a rocking chair.
> It gives you something to do but
> it doesn't get you anywhere.
>
> ~ Van Wilder

The best way to keep your mental health from failing is to keep your mind stayed on Jesus. Pray in His name often. Trust Him in all things, and always - from birth to death. He sustains your life and keeps your soul. Your mind directs your actions, and it needs to remain in good health at all times. You see, when you lose your mind, when it moves to the status of brain-dead, your body becomes non-functional. You no longer exist.

Worrying about things you have no control over is not a healthy state to be in. Do not give permission for anything or anyone to contaminate your mind with foolishness, causing it to be diseased beyond repair. There is always a point of no return, and you don't even want to go there. There are people who allow their minds to become so ill that they look for a way out through drugs or any other route that allows them to escape out of the plane of reality. They dress themselves in a parachute and jump out of the moving plane hoping to land safely in the land of **"never suffer any more"**, only to discover that there was a defect in the parachute, and they end up crashing to their death. The reality of life is the fact that we all will have troubles and tribulations on this road of life. But the mental protection we have is knowing that the Lord will deliver through every trial, whether it is physical or mental. Do not issue any permits for anything or anybody other than God to take over your mind or cause your mental condition to fail!

"Many are the afflictions of the righteous: but the Lord delivereth him out of them all. He keepeth all his bones: not one of them is broken." Psalm 34:19-20 (KJV)

Now let's talk about issuing permits for failure in physical health. Just because you become ill, it does not mean that God has something against you or that He is punishing you for past sins. God loves you and want nothing more than to have you in good health. He wants you well - He wants you to be at your best - He wants you to look good and feel good. God did not issue you a permanent certificate of good health when you were born. When you became of age and responsible for the stewardship of your own body, He expected you to make and keep your own doctor's appointments; eat the right foods; get enough rest; drink plenty of water; exercise your body and stay away from harmful activities that put your health at risk.

"Beloved, I wish above all things that thou mayest prosper and be in health, even as thy soul prospereth." ~ *3 John 1:2 (KJV)*

You live in a rented house - your body is a temple for the Holy Spirit to dwell in, and one day you will be required to move out. But in the meantime, you have to be responsible for the upkeep of your physical health. Do not issue any permits for your health to be compromised by outside sources, such as: illicit sexual encounters, over eating at smorgasbords, eating too many starches, and the list goes on with inappropriate eating habits. Do not allow anyone to convince you that it's ok for you to do anything harmful to your physical health or your body in any way.

Do not expect God to be responsible for keeping you in good health, even if you pray to Him for guidance. You have a responsibility to your own self. You have to know what season your health is in and handle it accordingly. Yes, God speaks to us in many ways when we pray to Him for help in maintaining our health, but sometimes He doesn't say anything. He expects you to take ownership and not issue any permits for your health to spiral down into a winter season. Bishop Millicent Hunter quotes in her book, *"Don't Die in the Winter: "Sometimes, God is silent. He does not appear to be moving or answering our prayers. Even during these times, the power and presence of God are with us in a powerful way. They are often just different. Every season has a new level of preparation."* Yes, you have to **prepare** yourself **to take care** of yourself.

NO PERMITS ISSUED TODAY

You must care for your spirit and soul just as you would care for a car.

- Get your soul inspected so all can see your goodness.
- Tune up your spiritual engine by reading the Word.
- Keep gas in your spiritual tank to run properly.
- Get gassed up by attending your church services and meetings regularly.
- Use quality gas— which is good and lively worship.
- Get your soul washed often in the blood of Jesus.
- Rotate your tires by praising God in the dance.
- Only carry passengers who will help keep you nice and clean. Don't let just anybody ride you.
- If the Holy Ghost pulls you over for driving too fast, He only wants to warn you before you crash.
- You should never smoke or drive and drink.
- No texting while driving.
- Look both ways before you cross an intersection of temptation.
- Get your spiritual oil changed when needed.
- Carry your owner's card with you at all times. God owns you—It is proven in the Bible.

- When it's rainy, Jesus will be your windshield wipers and He will wipe all tears from your eyes.
- Your praise will keep the air fresh inside of you.
- Remember to lock the doors when you get out, so the thief, Satan, won't steal you.
- Make sure you never park in Satan's tow away zone.
- If you crash, God has an awesome repair shop, ready to put you back together again—*with no charge!*

Do not allow anything or anybody to have a permit causing your physical health to fail. Now, say out loud with me, **"No permits issued today for my health to fail!"**

Chapter 7
Don't Give Permission For...

... Your Joy to be Removed

Your joy is the feeling you get from great happiness. Joy gives you strength and confidence deep down in your heart. Joy is jubilation (triumph) on you. When that is removed - when it is no longer on you, there is not much left. Your joy is the light of everlasting life which lights up your soul. You are compelled to hold on to it and guard it with your life!

One day in your life, Joy appeared on your front step and rang your doorbell. It may have come through the knowledge of passing an exam in school; a new bike for

Christmas, a letter of acceptance for a new job, sitting at the wheel of your brand new car or the sight of your first child being born. Whatever the case, whatever the situation - you opened the door when you heard the bell ring and you gladly welcomed joy into your heart with opened arms. You took ownership of that joy, you cherished the moment you received it and never wanted to let it go.

Well, let me make you aware of the fact that the enemy is lurking about; watching you, plotting on ways he can take that joy away from you. He wants to weaken you through other people or resources with loneliness, sadness, bad news, depression, sickness, rumors, lies, rejection and so many other things.

Life happens, situations come, trouble invades and trials parade. Yes, these things all come to steal your joy.

In your dark cloud times, remember that God is larger than any trial, sickness, pain or sorrow you may face in this life. What you must do is become serious about your relationship with God, so that He can speak to your heart during these life situations. He is a very present help during your time of storms.

"God is our refuge and strength, a very present help in trouble. Psalm 46:1 (KJV)

In the midst of these state of affairs, you have to become a very present receiver of His protection, advice, counsel, love, mercy and grace. Just receive what He offers you during sad times.

Be cognizant that the enemy cannot remove your joy unless you give him permission. He can't touch it unless you issue him a permit. I challenge you to stand flat on your feet with me today and declare; "No Permits Issued Today!" You can't do anything about yesterday because it is gone, but you can take charge of your 'today'. You will never be able to step into tomorrow to do anything about that, because it's not yours yet. Actually, you will never be able to catch up with tomorrow, because when it arrives - tomorrow automatically becomes today. Handle your today by declaring that nothing or no one will remove your God-given joy!

Because of negative situations occurring in your life right now, you may feel as if you are living in a 'night-time space'. You have to endure that night time experience, this is true - but when you go through, go through knowing that your morning will come and when it comes, it's bringing a boat load of joy.

"For His anger endureth but a moment; in His favor is life: weeping may endure for a night, but joy cometh in the morning." Psalms 30:5 (KJV)

Your morning joy comes from the Lord - it's yours and nobody should be allowed to remove it from you. Hold on to your joy. Cherish it forever and allow it to carry you throughout your whole life.

Now, let's explore how you can maintain and increase your joy:

1. You have to recognize the obstacles preventing you from being joyful.
2. You must do everything within your power to disband those obstacles.
3. If you allow the Spirit of God to dwell richly within you, He brings wonderful fruit and one of the fruits is 'joy'. His joy brings strength; you're going to need plenty in this day and time (Nehemiah 8:10). Listen to the voice of the Holy Spirit and let Him guide you down the pathway of joyful experiences.
4. Allow this joy to create unshakable stability within you.
5. Allow your relationship with God to grow through regular attendance of Bible Study services and worship services. Make sure you attend for the right reasons - not for the purpose of socializing, entertainment, making friends or seeking a spouse. Develop an intense and pure relationship with God and you will never be disappointed

with the outcome.

6. Entertain yourself with fresh ideas to keep your joy popping. If you force yourself to live a hum-drum boring life, your joy will not survive for long.

7. Don't overload yourself with assignments and chores, filling your entire day with work and business. You leave no space for an enjoyable moment. Take time to smell the roses!

8. Family time is a great activation button for joy. Allow time for spending quality moments with your family. I find that it brings much joy to my heart when I call my elderly family members to just check on them and see how they are doing. Their response to my calls are indeed joyful!

9. Get into the presence of God, through prayer, praise and worship. "Thou wilt shew me the path of life: in thy presence is fulness of joy; at thy right hand there are pleasures for evermore." Psalm 16:11

BISHOP ROSETTE CONEY

Chapter 8
Don't Give Permission For...
... Your Feelings to Be Hurt

Your feelings are the emotional side of your character; they can soar to the highest heights or plummet to the lowest lows. They can make you look good or make you look bad. How your feelings fair is strictly up to you. You have the power to direct and control your emotions.

You can expose your feelings, causing them to go out among others naked which enables them to boost you or crush you to the ground - or you can dress your emotions in layers of clothing so that you will not feel the bitter winds of outside elements. The Bible tells us to be clothed in humility. When you humble yourself under the mighty care of God, He will lift you up high above the level of hurt feelings.

"... Yea, all of you be subject one to another, and be clothed with humility: for God resisteth the proud, and giveth grace to the humble. Humble yourselves therefore under the mighty hand of God, that He may exalt you in due time: Casting all your care upon Him; for He careth for you." Peter 5:5-7 (KJV)

I once heard a powerful speaker, Bishop Erwin Scofield say, "The pain in our lives comes for a purpose - it comes to buffet us, to keep us on our knees in fervent prayer". Like Apostle Paul sought the Lord three times and asked Him to remove the thorn from his side, but God politely declined and inspired him instead with the thought that His grace was sufficient. We have to realize that any attacks allowed to come against us were allowed by God and His grace will sufficiently take us through - hurt feelings and all. What helps is remembering that what doesn't kill us will make us strong. At no time should we relinquish our permission for attacks or negative statements to get the best of our feelings.

We sometimes put ourselves in positions to be hurt by extending our feelings, exposing them to hurtful people and those who impact our lives - or by sticking our noses in matters which really don't concern us. I would like to share with you my personal take on how to handle your hurt feelings:

1. Get a clear understanding of why your feelings were hurt in the first place.
2. Get a hold of your emotions.
3. Don't forget who you are and Whose you are.
4. Don't let the enemy know that he hurt you.
5. Practice minding your own business.
6. Don't try to force people to live their lives your way.
7. When your feelings start hurting, start praising the God who heals you! "He healeth the broken in heart, and bindeth up their wounds." (Psalms 147:3)
8. Keep in the front of your mind the insults Jesus sustained on His way to the cross; some even coming from His closest friends and the crowd who - only days before His horrific crucifixion, celebrated Him with their praises and cries of "Hosanna".
9. When someone hurts your feelings, don't try to avenge yourself. God will fight your battles for you and He can do a much better job than you ever could.
10. When your feelings are hurt, press forward even harder

than before they were hurt. This will take the wind out of the enemy's sail.

11. Do not relinquish your right to feel good about yourself. Speak from your mouth positive affirmations of love, joy and peace. You can find all of these in the Word of God.

12. Focus on your blessings. You are blessed beyond measure and God has even greater blessings ahead of you.

13. Develop a spirit of forgiveness; this will become easier as you decide not to let 'un-forgiveness' make you a prisoner. Let past hurts stay in the past.

14. Envelop everything in a prayer. Pray, then pray some more until you begin to feel better about your pain.

When you truly think about it, hurt feelings are something everyone experiences at some point. It's a place we have all visited, but we didn't have to stay there permanently. Just keep it moving.

You can't always blame other people when your feelings get hurt. You have to take ownership of your feelings. The feelings are your own. You never say, "Your feelings were hurt when you didn't invite me to your party!" You say, "My feelings were hurt when you didn't invite me to your party!" In order for you to be hurt, you have to give them permission. Now, what are you going to do with that!?

You have to acknowledge and admit that your feelings were hurt and assume the task of healing those feelings, using some of the techniques mentioned earlier in this writing. If you don't do something about it, those feelings will become a big ball in your stomach and create an even larger problem. Just don't issue any permits for your feelings to continue taking charge of your life - don't bathe in the hurt. Instead, bathe in your healing!

"For we have not a high priest which cannot be touched with the feeling of our infirmities; but was in all points tempted like as we are, yet without sin. Let us therefore come boldly unto the throne of grace, that we may obtain mercy, and find grace to help in time of need."

Hebrews 4:15-16 (KJV)

It is quite comforting to know that we have a Savior who is connected to the feelings we have and we can always go to Him for strength and grace to deal with our discomfort and pain. With the knowledge of that powerful throne of grace, we can boldly enter in, torn and battered and come out strong and brave with enough authority to cancel all previously issued permits. Now say aloud with me, *"No permits issued today to hurt my feelings!"*

Chapter 9
Don't Give Permission For...

... Your Smile to Be Reversed

Your smile is a reflection of your personality. A smile is what forms a person's features into a pleasant, kind expression, typically with the corners of the mouth turned upward; which I say points to heaven and God. When those same corners of the mouth are turned down, the mouth forms a frown and points downward - which I say, to hell and the devil. I might add that a frown is the reversed action of a smile.

When you smile at others, it tells them very clearly that you acknowledge them and also approve them. You can never deny how good it feels to give and receive a smile, especially when you're having a bad day. People never expect harm from a smiling person. A smile makes everyone feel good, secure and comfortable. God gave you that smile and you should never permit anyone, any situation or circumstance cause your smile to be reversed. It's been said that when you smile, the whole world smiles with you – but when you frown, you frown alone.

Smiles also express humility and submissiveness. A smile is a facial welcome sign showing that you are approachable. Smiles are significant because…

- they promote peace
- they are calming
- they remove strain and stress
- they make your voice sound happier when you speak
- they make you think positive

A reversed smile is of course, a frown. Frowns express dissatisfaction, discomfort or pain and can be brought on by a number of resources. One thing for sure, frowns expressed on your face may be excused due to bad smells of garbage; in sympathy of the pain others experience, pain in your body or an illness - but certainly not frowns generated from outside influences, like judgment passed onto others or from other negative pressure points.

Do not allow anyone or anything to reverse your happy day. Start your day with a smile on your face and a song in your heart. Smile and sing because you're happy - smile and sing because you're free. It's good to know that just like God's eyes are on the sparrow, you got to know He's watching over you too!

Some things in your day may go wrong - this is true, but a great big old smile on your face will change direction of your bad day. The late Nat King Cole used to sing a song which expresses my sentiments exactly and it goes something like this...

Smile though your heart is aching
Smile even though it's breaking
When there are clouds in the sky, you'll get by
If you smile through your fear and sorrow
Smile and maybe tomorrow
You'll see the sun come shining through for you

Light up your face with gladness
Hide every trace of sadness
Although a tear may be ever so near
That's the time you must keep on trying
Smile, what's the use of crying?
You'll find that life is still worthwhile

If you just smile

That's the time you must keep on trying
Smile, what's the use of crying?
You'll find that life is still worthwhile
If you just smile

Yes, smile and don't give any permits for that smile to be turned upside down. You just keep on smiling through every test and every trial. You've got smiley angels positioned right there on the ends of your lips holding those corners up through every painful moment that dares to appear in your life.

Sometimes our smiles are stolen from us by people I call, 'illegal attachments'.

We attach ourselves to toxic people who become bloodsucking leaches. They hold on to us for dear life. They steal our smiles. They become a weight and eventually a sin.

The Bible tells us to lay aside every weight and the sin that does so easily beset us and run with patience the race set before us. It also tells us Who to look to for help; we must look to Jesus.

There are three illegal attachments which generally hold us back from smiling and from reaching the highest potential already designed for us. They are:
- Those who **need us** to fulfill their needs...
- Those who are **assigned by the enemy** to destroy us...
- Those who **we feel we need** in our lives to be happy.

I'm told that 'Happy' is a place we are only supposed to visit, not dwell. Happy is not supposed to have permanent residence within us. If we attach ourselves to someone or something we believe we need in order to be happy, we are setting ourselves up for a terrible travesty.

The Bible also says weeping may endure for a night, but joy comes in the morning - but guess what follows that joy again? More weeping and it goes on and on and on and on; the cycle never ends until we are in the grave.

"Man that is born of a woman is of few days, and full of trouble. He cometh forth like a flower, and is cut down: he fleeth also as a shadow, and continueth not." Job 14:1-2 (KJV)

We were born into a world of trouble. When we were flushed from the birth canal, the only thing attached to us was the umbilical cord. When we die, we die naked – we cannot take things with us nor people.

Now, let's review those three illegal attachments again:

1. The attachments who cling to us to fulfill their needs, drain the very life from us. They are people who often arrange our schedules around themselves. They call us on the phone excessively or text us repeatedly. What makes these individuals illegal is the fact they <u>leave no time for us to spend with God.</u> God wants our minds to remain on Him, therefore anyone who intercepts that arrangement is in the eyes of God, **illegal**. Open your mouth right now and say, **"That's illegal!"**

2. The next illegal attachments are those who assigned to us by the devil. We can't get rid of these attachments; they come to kill, steal and destroy. They pretend they are in our corner, while keeping us in a corner. They smile in our faces and stab us behind our backs. They operate illegally, because God did not assign them to us. Open your mouth right now and say, "That's illegal!"

3. The last illegal attachments are the ones we depend on to make us happy. We view them through a curtain of needs, covered with a cloth of wants and desires. We chase after them instead of chasing after God. We rely on them to fulfill our dreams and hopes. This is indeed an illegal attachment. God says, "I am a jealous God." Open your mouth right now and say, "That's illegal!"

Our only LEGAL attachment is the Lord our God. He's the One who says cling to Me - I will be your Father and you shall be my sons and daughters. He promised to be everything you need!

Do not issue permits to these illegal attachments who only come around to reverse your smiles. Tell all of your illegals, they have been detached! Tell the devil; *"You no longer have control over me! You have been detached! You are an illegal alien and you have to go!"*

God has a plan for your life which attaches you only to Him. We are attached to God. We can't see Him, but we can feel Him moving inside of us and in times of trouble, He is going to hide us in His secret place. The Bible says in 2 Corinthians 4:18; "While we look not at the things which are seen, but at the things which are not seen: for the things which are seen are temporal; but the things which are not seen are eternal.

You declare with your mouth right now, ***"If it's illegal I don't want any part of it!*** What God has for me, it is for me!" Just shake the stuff off today. There is no room in your life or illegal stuff. No more permits for these kinds of things! The Bible encourages us to lay aside every encumbrance and the sin which so easily entangles us and let us run with endurance the race that is set before us.

"Be ye not unequally yoked together with unbelievers: for what fellowship hath righteousness with unrighteousness? And what communion hath light with darkness? And what concord hath Christ with Belial? or what part hath he that believeth with an infidel? And what agreement hath the temple of God with idols? for ye are the temple of the living God; as God hath said, I will dwell in them, and walk in them ; and I will be their God, and they shall be my people. Wherefore come out from among them, and be ye separate, saith the Lord, and touch not the unclean thing ; and I will receive you, And will be a Father

unto you, and ye shall be my sons and daughters, saith the Lord Almighty." 2 Corinthians 6:14-18 (KJV)

All of the illegal people, places and things in your life must go! They are not your equal. You've have to just let them go and let them go today!!!! Yes, let them go and turn your dark light back on again - this will get your smile back!

See
My
Inner
Light
Excel

Now say with me out loud, ***"No permits issued today that will reverse my smile!"***

BISHOP ROSETTE CONEY

Chapter 10
Don't Give Permission For...

... Your Blessings to Be Blocked

There's a blessing with your name written on it and you don't want to issue permits for it to be blocked. A blessing is anything connected to God's favor and protection. Your blessing can range from a good doctor's report to a brand new car. God blesses how He desires to bless, who He desires to bless and when He desires to bless - but His blessings are conditional.

"And all these blessings shall come on thee, and overtake thee, if thou shalt hearken unto the voice of the Lord thy God." Deuteronomy 28:2

Your blessings are sitting on the edge of heaven's gates, waiting to pour out like a shower of rain onto you. If I were you, I wouldn't issue any permits for them to be blocked by anybody or anything - no, not today!

When something is blocked it is hindered, the flow of it is stopped; a wall of bricks is built so that one cannot see or proceed past the wall.

The blessings of Abraham, Isaac and Jacob are just as effective today as they were in the days of old. All of these individuals received their specific, identifiable, custom-made blessings from God specifically because of their incredible, unshakeable faith in His ability to come through for them. Because they pleased God (without faith it is impossible to please Him) their blessings were far from being blocked. As a matter of fact, He was their Rewarder of abundant blessings.

"But without faith it is impossible to please Him: for he that cometh to God must believe that He is, and that He is a rewarder of them that diligently seek Him." Hebrews 11:6

Your blessings stand in danger of being blocked by your worst enemy – Satan. He wants to do all he can to kill, steal and destroy your blessings by any means necessary. He comes disguised in sheep's clothing. He looks good, smells good and talks good, but he's a raging wolf underneath the sheep's wool. He wants you to become disobedient to God, His Word and His leaders. He knows that your blessings will be blocked if you step into the cloak room of disobedience. He wants you to be obnoxious to those who have rule over you in the Lord or in your work place. He wants you to be self-righteous and self-centered, desiring to have things go your way in your church, in your home, on your job and among your family members. He doesn't care when, he doesn't care where, he doesn't care how and he doesn't care who he uses to get you to buck up against God's standards and directives. He doesn't care that this is blocking your blessings - he just wants you to be miserably empty and discouraged; especially when you see others being blessed around you. Do not issue any permits to let this happen!

Let's explore some ways in which you can free your blocked blessings:

WALK IN GOD'S STATUTES

❖ Leviticus 26:3-10 - *"If ye walk in my statutes, and keep my commandments, and do them;Then I will give you rain in due season, and the land shall yield her increase, and the trees of the field shall yield their fruit. And your threshing shall reach unto the vintage, and the vintage shall reach unto the sowing time: and ye shall eat your bread to the full, and dwell in your land safely. And I will give peace in the land, and ye shall lie down, and none shall make you afraid: and I will rid evil beasts out of the land, neither shall the sword go through your land. And ye shall chase your enemies, and they shall fall before you by the sword. And five of you shall chase an hundred, and an hundred of you shall put ten thousand to flight: and your enemies shall fall before you by the sword. For I will have respect unto you, and make you fruitful, and multiply you, and establish my covenant with you. And ye shall eat old store, and bring forth the old because of the new."*

FEAR THE LORD

❖ Deuteronomy 6:24 - *"And the Lord commanded us to do all these statutes, to fear the Lord our God, for our good always, that he might preserve us alive, as it is at this day."*

OBEY THE LORD YOUR GOD

- ❖ Deuteronomy 28:1-2 -*"And it shall come to pass, if thou shalt hearken diligently unto the voice of the Lord thy God, to observe and to do all his commandments which I command thee this day, that the Lord thy God will set thee on high above all nations of the earth: And all these blessings shall come on thee, and overtake thee, if thou shalt hearken unto the voice of the Lord thy God."*

DEPEND ON THE LORD FOR EVERYTHING

- ❖ Deuteronomy 30:9-10 - *"And the Lord thy God will make thee plenteous in every work of thine hand, in the fruit of thy body, and in the fruit of thy cattle, and in the fruit of thy land, for good: for the Lord will again rejoice over thee for good, as he rejoiced over thy fathers: If thou shalt hearken unto the voice of the Lord thy God, to keep his commandments and his statutes which are written in this book of the law, and if thou turn unto the Lord thy God with all thine heart, and with all thy soul."*

BE WILLING TO OBEY

- ❖ Isaiah 1:19 -*"If ye be willing and obedient, ye*

shall eat the good of the land"

Listen, as a child of the Most High God, you and your descendants have a right to be blessed. It's one of the benefits that come with being an obedient child. Bask in those blessings! Wake up every morning expecting blessings. Go to bed with great anticipation of receiving more blessings as the sun rises the next day. Open your mouth and say with me, **"There will be no permits issued today to block my blessings!"**

Chapter 11
Don't Give Permission For...

... *Your Mind to Be Polluted*

Your mind is the element which enables you to be aware of the world and your experiences, to think and to fear; the faculty of conscientiousness and thought. It is your intellect, your intelligence, your capabilities and brain power. When that part of you is polluted, your whole world is messed up. Pollution is contamination, tainting. It is the presence in or introduction into the environment of a substance or thing that has harmful or poisonous effects.

The mind is similar to a computer's CPU (central processing unit). Your mind processes everything that involves you. You actually become what you think.

"For as he thinketh in his heart, so is he:…"

Proverbs 23:7a (KJV)

Your mind is your most powerful commodity because it is connected to your soul. With your mind connected to your soul, you create a divine matrix. The matrix is material in which something develops a surrounding medium or structure. Your mind joins your soul and tells your sick body that you are healed! They join together again and tell your empty wallet that it's full. We live in a time when the word of God is still as powerful as it was in the days of old. We become what we develop in or minds - we are only more than a conqueror if we think we are.

At all costs, we have to protect our minds. We can't afford to leave any doors or windows of our minds opened for Satan to enter in and cause destruction. He comes in like a thief - to steal, kill and destroy. There are several tools Satan uses to sneak upon us.

- Drugs or substance abuse
- Abuse of alcohol
- Illicit sexual desires
- Low self-esteem
- Depression
- Confusion
- Rejection

- Peer pressure
- Illnesses
- Idleness
- Unemployment
- Jealousy
- Hatred

All of these things are birthed in the mind. I want you to know that you do not have to let Satan use you like a puppet. You don't have to let him gain entrance - come in, or wreak havoc in your head. Do not issue him a permit to take over and pollute your mind. In the Bible, Judas issued a permit for Satan to enter his mind and he ended up betraying our Lord and Savior, Jesus Christ. Satan was issued a permit to enter Peter's mind and he denied knowing Christ three times.

Cain issued a permit for Satan to enter his mind and he became jealous of his brother and killed him. This invasion always has a point of no return. Once the damage is done it's hard to undo the destruction. When a life is lost, you can't bring it back. When relationships are damaged or polluted, the repair job can become absolutely hopeless.

The prodigal son issued a permit to Satan and allowed

him to enter his mind. He was moved to leave the comfort of his family home to live a riotous life of wasting his money, traveling 'from glory to the gutter.' He made the shocking discovery of what happens when you issue Satan a permit to pollute your mind. Your mind dictates your actions. You can't even move your hand without the permission of your mind. You can't walk, talk, eat or speak with your mind all jacked up. It doesn't take much to pollute it; all it takes is an open slit for the enemy to slither his way in.

So then, let's discuss what is required to shut down the avenues that compel you to issue permits which cause your mind to be polluted.

1. You have to scream out loud and decree that no permits will be issued to touch your mind or thoughts. Job 22:28 reads, *"Thou shalt also decree a thing, and it shall be established unto thee: and the light shall shine upon thy ways."* After you decree this thing, pray and ask God to help you believe that it shall be done and mentally start walking in faith.
2. Check out your mind to see what war is occurring that causes you to issue permits for contamination. Check it out and see what you are thinking, see how you are thinking and determine if you are even thinking at all.

Romans 7:23 reads; *"But I see another law in my members, warring against the law of my mind, and bringing me into captivity to the law of sin which is in my members."*

3. Once you discover that your mind has been besieged, taken over, contaminated or polluted; do whatever is necessary to get it running properly. Get yourself together! Your mind is in direct communication with your affections or devotion. Your mind is going to serve that which you are devoted to. If your mind has been polluted with the things of this earth, which takes over your entire being - free yourself by hitting the 'reset button' and do this immediately! You have no time to waste! Colossians 3:2 reads; *"Set your affection on things above, not on things on the earth."* In other words, you have to set your mind on things higher than where you are in your mind while here on earth; heavenly things, things of love, peace and joy - uplifting things. Romans12:2 (ESV) also encourages you to hit the reset button; *"Do not be conformed to this world, but be transformed by the renewal of your mind, that by testing you may discern what is the will of God, what is good and acceptable and perfect."* You can also plunge into your mental strength by internalizing Philippians

4:8-9; *"Finally, brethren, whatsoever things are true, whatsoever things are honest, whatsoever things are just, whatsoever things are pure, whatsoever things are lovely, whatsoever things are of good report; if there be any virtue, and if there be any praise, **think on these things**. Those things, which ye have both learned, and received, and heard, and seen in me, do: and the God of peace shall be with you."*

4. Finally, get yourself a mental transplant; the process of moving from a stinking thinking prison cell into a positive, purified, powerful mind of freedom. Take on the mind of Christ. 1st Corinthians 2:16 reads; *"For who hath known the mind of the Lord, that he may instruct him? But we have the mind of Christ."*

5. Also a powerful verse to lasso is Philippians 2:5, which gives a directive that will keep you from issuing permits to anything or anyone desiring to pollute your mind. *"Let this mind be in you, which was also in Christ Jesus:"* Jesus did not allow anything to rise in His mind that would prevent Him from doing the will of His Father. You already have what it takes to be in control of maintaining a clean and untainted mind, if the Spirit of God lives within you. 1st John 4:4 reads; *"Ye are of God, little children, and have overcome them: because greater*

is he that is in you, than he that is in the world."

So get busy and conquer the power or source that is knocking on the door of your mind for a permit; conquer it without fear, conquer it with confidence - conquer it in the name of Jesus! You have power, you have love and you have a sound mind right now as you read this! Why, because God has not given you the spirit of fear, but of power, love and a sound mind (*2nd Timothy 1:7*). Now, open your mouth and say with me, **"No permits will be issued today to pollute my mind!"**

Chapter 12
Don't Give Permission For...

... *Your Vision to Be Aborted*

Your vision is your ability to perceive, create, dream, produce or expand in a desired area. The sky is the limit. Your vision allows you to reach beyond the stars and if your vision is plugged into the socket called 'the will of God', you will receive provision to carry out your vision. Your needs will be met physically, mentally and financially. There is a vision conceived inside of you. If you issue a permit for that vision to be aborted, it will never be birthed.

"Being confident of this very thing, that he which hath begun a good work in you will perform it until the day of

Jesus Christ" Philippians 1:6 (KJV)

Now let's talk about that vision, the good thing God planted in you! Let's talk about the seed planted by your Creator. In you, God has planted a seed of success, waiting to be watered, nurtured and warmed by the sun (Son).

I bet you didn't know that the watering of the seed comes from the tears you shed from discouragement, pain, sorrow, disappointments, rejections, abuse; all of those things were contributive factors in the production of your vision. They weren't allowed to distract or destroy you. They were sent to push you into your greatness.

- There's a song inside of you, waiting to be recorded
- There's a book inside of you, waiting to be written
- There's a business inside of you, waiting to be launched
- There's a Word inside of you, waiting to be preached
- There's an invention inside of you, waiting to be discovered
- There's a painting inside of you, waiting to be placed on a canvass

All of these things are birthed through trials and tribulations - some things given, some things taken away. Also, there will be some things gained, some things lost. Some things require you to pick up and some things you must put down.

Some people come into your life to help you, some come into your life to hurt you. These things and people are not intended to push you into issuing a permit to abort your vision, but to inspire your creative juices to go forth. I once read a quote from someone who must have had a direct connection with God in order to think of such a powerful statement. The quote simply says:

"God will never leave you empty. He will replace everything you lost. If He asks you to put something down, it's because He wants you to pick up something greater."

This statement brings it all together. You just have to trust God in all things and include in your prayers and cries of hopelessness unto the Lord this statement; "Father, God, what would You have me to learn from this bad experience?" He will provide an answer, even if it's something you don't want to hear. God loves you emphatically and only want what's best for you. The bright-lighted vision He placed inside of you shines the brightest during your darkest hour. As you go through the process of learning how to master the art of trusting Him more, don't be afraid to lean forward into your vision. To avoid the abortion of your vision, consider these tips:

❖ Write the vision down.

- ❖ Read it to yourself over and over again.
- ❖ Purchase what you need to start the vision. Remember that God provides provision for the vision.
- ❖ Abandon fear - fear comes from the devil. Faith comes from reading and hearing God's Word.
- ❖ Ask God for wisdom and the ability to discern who you can trust sharing your vision with. Remember there are vision crushers waiting with instruments of destruction to abort the vision.
- ❖ Prepare yourself to invest in your own vision first. Don't become a beggar - when some people give to you, they think they own you. Don't let that happen. Be smart enough to open a savings account to fund your own vision with God's help.
- ❖ Paint your vision with prayer. Pray, then pray some more. Thank God in your prayer for provisions for the vision and thank Him for its manifestation even before it's fulfilled. *"And whatever you ask in prayer, you will receive, if you have faith."* (Proverbs 21:22 ESV)
- ❖ Make sure that your vision is a God-inspired vision and not a trick from Satan. You can always tell because the Bible says, **"The blessing of the Lord, it maketh rich, and He addeth no sorrow with it."** (Proverbs 10:22 KJV)

- ❖ Finally, get that vision and run with it!

    "And the Lord answered me, and said,

    Write the vision, and make it plain upon tables,

    that he may run that readeth it.

    For the vision is yet for an appointed time,

    but at the end it shall speak, and not lie:

    though it tarry, wait for it;

    because it will surely come, it will not tarry."

    Habakkuk 2:2-3

    God has impregnated you with something wonderful! You have something marvelous growing inside of you. Every so often, it will give you a big kick to get you moving in the right direction. Don't become lazy about pulling things together for your vision.

    - o Plan a baby shower for that vision. Celebrate it before it comes to full fruition.
    - o Go shopping for spiritual food and necessary items to make it nice.
    - o Send out invitations to those who don't mind celebrating the vision with you.
    - o Get excited about the vision.
    - o Make sure you have a place for the vision to dwell when it comes.
    - o Do all you can to keep yourself in good shape while

you wait.

Don't let anything or anybody stop you or cause you to end the delivery of that vision.

Go forth with your vision, and your plans will be established - just go forth and say with me, "*No permits will be issued today to abort my vision!*"

"Commit your work to the Lord, and your plans will be established." Proverbs 16:3 (ESV)

Chapter 13
Don't Give Permission For...

... Your Heart to Be Discouraged

In the natural sense, your heart is the hollow muscular organ that pumps blood through the circulatory system by rhythmic contraction and dilation. In vertebrates there are four chambers (as in humans), with two atria and two ventricles. You can't live without your heart. Your heart is the seat of your emotions; it is the center of your thoughts and emotions, especially love or compassion. When it is discouraged, it can shut down your whole system.

Your heart can be discouraged in so many ways, so it's imperative that you keep it securely safe from hurt, harm and danger. "Keep your heart with all vigilance, for from it flow the springs of life." Proverbs 4:23 (ESV)

Disappointments in life can cause one's heart to become discouraged. Sadness appears when you are discouraged and when your spirits sink low, it will take more than a powerful crane to raise them. When your heart has been hurt, major emotional surgery has to occur. Bishop Millicent created a cure for the pains of a heartache in her book, *How to Survive a Hurt Attack.* She developed a 'Life Clinic' that outlines the remedy for survival. Bishop Hunter shares how you must do your *headwork* and the *heart work* in order to survive a hurt attack. To survive the pain of discouragement that comes with a hurt attack thrown at your heart - you must be a believer, you must want God's will for your life, you must forgive others and you must not pray or speak affirmations with selfish motives. Bishop further confirms that you have to want to be a survivor!

Might I suggest the following things you should maintain in order to keep your heart from becoming discouraged:

- *Hold on to your joy*
- *Trust God without wavering*
- *Allow God the time it takes to remove the damaged heart*
- *Stay away from people who continue to discourage your*

heart

- *Stay light hearted*
- *Fall head over hills in love with God*
- *Allow God to try your heart*
- *Watch what you say to others*

❖ Hold on to your joy, because it will be your strength to make it through the disappointing stages of your life. *"A joyful heart is good medicine, but a crushed spirit dries up the bones."* Proverbs 17:22 (ESV)

❖ Trust God without wavering in your faith. Without faith, you cannot please God. If you ever needed to please anybody, it is indeed Him. He is the One who can supply all your needs. *"Trust in the Lord with all your heart, and do not lean on your own understanding."* Proverbs 3:5 (ESV)

❖ Allow God the time it takes to remove the damaged heart. God works on His own time. He is not at all moved by your complaints and impatience. He knows the plans that He has for you and the new heart of flesh He wants to put inside of you is discourage-proofed; *"And I will give you a new heart, and a new spirit I will put within you. And I will remove the heart of stone from your flesh and give you a heart of flesh."* Ezekiel 36:26 (ESV)

- <u>Stay away from people</u> who continue to discourage your heart. There are people with evil intent, laying hard on your doorbell, wanting to enter your heart, wine and dine you and then rip your heart apart. Do not let that happen - do not issue any permits for discouragement from these types of people. They take joy in your pain. Ask God for wisdom and discernment to see these traps ahead of time. Don't fall for fake lovers or friends who plan and plot for ways to hurt or discourage you. *"For he is like one who is inwardly calculating. "Eat and drink!" he says to you, but his heart is not with you."* Proverbs 23:7 (ESV)

- <u>Stay light hearted</u>. Laugh your way through hurtful situations. Keep yourself relaxed and free from worry. Worry causes stress and anxiety. Don't take some things so seriously; those things that weigh down your heart can sometimes cause a physical heart attack. *"Anxiety in a man's heart weighs him down, but a good word makes him glad."* Proverbs 12:25 (ESV)

- <u>Fall head over heels in love with God</u> - this is the best thing you could ever do. When you allow yourself to fall deeply in love with God, you learn to trust Him no matter what. When you love Him - and I mean truly love Him, you actually feel Him loving you right back. One of the by-products of your love is your obedience and another manifestation is your worship. The love God offers you pads you so thickly, that you will never feel the brutish attacks which normally cause your heart to become discouraged. *"And he said to him, "You shall love the Lord your God with all your heart and with all your soul and with all your mind."* Matthew 22:37 (ESV)

- ❖ Allow God to try your heart. When your heart is tested, it enables you to see how weak or strong you are - it allows God to see this as well. Ask God to search your heart and if there's anything which should not be there - pray and ask your Heavenly Father to perform an operation of removal so that your salvation will not be hampered. Only the pure in heart will see God. *"Search me, O God, and know my heart! Try me and know my thoughts! And see if there be any grievous way in me, and lead me in the way everlasting!"* Psalms 139:23-24 (ESV)

- ❖ Watch what you say to others. Your mouth could get you into trouble and cause you to bring discouragement upon yourself. Pray and ask God to choose your words for you. There is a passage of scripture in the Bible which declares that death and life are in the power of the tongue. (Proverbs 18:21 KJV) The words served from your own mouth may have to be eaten by you ultimately. *"Let the words of my mouth and the meditation of my heart be acceptable in your sight, O Lord, my rock and my redeemer."* Psalms 19:14 (ESV) Open your mouth and say with me right now, **"No permits will be issued for my heart to be discouraged today!"**

Chapter 14
Don't Give Permission For...
... *Your Past to Infect Your Future*

Your past can be defined as the failures in your life and mistakes made that prevent you from moving forward successfully and create a poisonous venom keeping you in a depressed prison cell. Any negative components of your past can dangerously infect (spread a disease to) your future in many ways:

- Problems finding a job
- Difficulty in maintaining a relationship with spouse or significant other

- Insecurity and Trust issues
- Low Self Esteem
- Health issues

It will be difficult for you to press forward into the future while looking at the past. The past represents what used to be. The present represents what is and can direct what your future holds. The future represents something to look forward to. If you are persistent in hovering in the past, you could become lost in situations which could have devastating results. Let us review some issues of your past that could infect your future:

Problems finding a job:

- If you believe you will never amount to being the person an employer is looking for to fill a position, then you will complete an application with an already-defeated mentality.
- Your potential employer will have problems with you when it comes to criticism. You will base all criticism on the fact that you had a bad situation in your past life which holds you back from progressing.
- Do not allow your past failures to keep you from succeeding and finding employment. Forget about the past. God is ready and willing to do a new thing in you.

"Remember not the former things, nor consider the

things of old. Behold, I am doing a new thing; now it springs forth, do you not perceive it? I will make a way in the wilderness and rivers in the desert." Isaiah 43:18-19 (ESV)

Difficulty in maintaining a relationship with spouse or significant other:
- The pain you suffered in past bad relationships may carry over into your new relationships or marriage, causing many problems for the poor souls you end up with.
- There are usually several bursts of unexplained crying, mood swings and other strange behavior patterns when you suffer from the memory of a previous bad relationship.
- Where abuse occurred in the past, there is usually fear-filled luggage carried into new relationships.
- Pray and ask God to help you rely on His Word for healing in situations like this and do not let a bad past relationship infect the future with your spouse or significant other. *"Thou wilt keep him in perfect peace, whose mind is stayed on thee: because he trusteth in thee. Trust ye in the Lord forever: for in the Lord Jehovah is everlasting strength:"* Isaiah 26:3-4
- Your past should not be the power source that determines

your future. God holds the future and He heals past wounds in a manner that produces complete emotional healing now and in the future.

Low Self-Esteem

- This comes from thinking poorly of yourself, especially when comparing yourself to other people who have accomplished more then you, who are more beautiful than you or who has more money than you, etc.
- Low self-esteem is a very debilitating contaminant. When it enters your system, it can cut you off from the rest of the world. It's always you against the world.
- To raise yourself self-esteem, you have to use your past failures and build a high platform on which to stand. When you stand on that platform, you will be able to look to the hills from where your help comes - it comes from the Lord. David said in Psalm 121:1-2, *"I will lift up mine eyes unto the hills, from whence cometh my help. My help cometh from the Lord, which made heaven and earth."*
- Instead of hiding and burying yourself in your dark past, using it as an excuse to act out of character - just emerge into a bright future, using Jesus as a light to show you the way. He is the light of the whole world.

Health Issues (mental or physical)

- When God heals you from sicknesses which plagued your body in the past, walk in that new-found healing. Don't look back and take on the pain again, claiming it as though it still exists. Let it go! You are a new creation in Christ.
- If you were molested in the past, damaged in your mind of that violation from a loved one, family friend or stranger - move from that space in your head and walk in the newness of life.
- Don't hold on to past hurts and pains - if you do, it will take you down a path that leads to no end. Before you know it, you'll be involved in corrupt activities in a failed attempt to mask your pain. Shut down that train of thought and declare within yourself you will not issue any permits to let your past destroy or infect your future.

"To put off your old self, which belongs to your former manner of life and is corrupt through deceitful desires, and to be renewed in the spirit of your minds, and to put on the new self, created after the likeness of God in true righteousness and holiness."

Ephesians 4:22-23

Decide within yourself that you are going to thrust forward into your bright future, forgetting those things which are behind you. Keep going forward, looking to Jesus, who is the Author and Finisher of your faith. Stand tall with me and speak now out of your mouth the declaration: *"I will not be issuing a permit today for my past to infect my future!"*

NO PERMITS ISSUED TODAY

Scriptural Encouragement for Strength

BISHOP ROSETTE CONEY

In conclusion, here are some comforting scriptures to assist in your journey of gaining your strength back, as you shut down the issuance all of permits today…

STRENGTH WILL NOT SWIM OUT TO YOU – YOU HAVE TO SWIM OUT TO IT!

- **Psalm 105:4** - *"Seek the LORD, and His strength: seek His face evermore."*

- **1 Chronicles 16:11** - *"Seek the LORD and His strength, seek His face continually."*

YOU HAVE TO HOLD ON TO A ROCK TO SYMBOLIZE THE PRESENCE OF GOD.
- **Psalms 62:7** – *"In God is my salvation and my glory: the rock of my strength, and my refuge, is in God."*

WHEN YOU ARE AT YOUR WORSE, THAT'S WHEN HE IS AT HIS BEST TO PERFECT YOU.

- **2 Corinthians 12:9** - *"And he said unto me, My*

grace is sufficient for thee: for my strength is made perfect in weakness. Most gladly therefore will I rather glory in my infirmities, that the power of Christ may rest upon me."

- o **2 Samuel 22:33** - *"God is my strength and __power__: and He maketh my way perfect."*

GOD HAS EVERYTHING YOU NEED TO BE STRONG – TRY LEANING ON HIM.

- o **1 Chronicles 29:12** - *"Both riches and honour come of thee, and thou reignest over all; and in thine hand is power and might; and in thine hand it is to make great, and to give strength unto all."*

WHEN YOUR HEART CAN'T TAKE IT ANYMORE, TRUST GOD – HE CAN TAKE IT!
- o **Psalm 73:26** - *"My flesh and my heart faileth: but God is the strength of my heart, and my portion forever."*

DO WHAT IT TAKES TO ENJOY THE LORD – GO TO CHURCH – THAT'S YOUR STRENGTH!

- **Nehemiah 8:10** *"...for the joy of the LORD is your strength."*

- **Psalms 28:7** - *"The LORD is my strength and my shield; my heart trusted in Him, and I am helped: therefore my heart greatly rejoiceth; and with my song will I praise Him."*

- Finally, read **2 Timothy 2:1-14**

I'm stronger now, so there will be No Permits Issued Today!

About the Author

Bishop Rosette Coney is the Senior Pastor of the Church of the Living God, in the Kensington section of Philadelphia, located at 2738 N. 2nd Street; and has extensive experience in leadership roles of the corporate world and the religious sector. She is the General Secretary for the national Church of the Living God, an active member of the Bethel Deliverance International Fellowship of Churches where she serves on the Holy Convocation Planning Committee, is the Chaplain of the Strawberry Mansion Faith Based Coalition, and a part of the Conference Team of the Baptist Worship Center.

Her passion is for ushering people into their greatness with inspiration, love and encouragement. She was honored in 2013 by Enon Tabernacle Baptist Church with the "Masters Award" for her demonstration of strong Christian character, principles, values and morals in life, while fighting the forces of evil. In 2016, she was awarded the Humanitarian Award by the *Beyond Expectations in Partnership with the NCBW* in the Essington Section of the City of Philadelphia.

She is a passionate wife for 46 years, a mother, grandmother, leader, teacher, friend, pastor, advisor, motivational speaker, professional singer, mentor, sister, author, artist - but ***enjoys most of all*** being a true servant of God.

Be sure to get her leadership book entitled, Take Your Feet Off the Seat. Her life-driven scripture is Philippians 4:13, *"I can do all things through Christ which strengtheneth me."*

NO PERMITS ISSUED TODAY

www.ingramcontent.com/pod-product-compliance
Lightning Source LLC
Chambersburg PA
CBHW070932160426
43193CB00011B/1664

9780998466545